Man with Bombe Alaska

Kate Behrens was born in 1959 with her late twin Sophie. Two Rivers Press published her first collection, *The Beholder*, in 2012. She lives in Oxfordshire and has one daughter.

Also by Two Rivers Poets:
David Attwooll, *The Sound Ladder* (2015)
Paul Bavister, *Miletree* (1996)
Paul Bavister, *Glass* (1998)
Paul Bavister, *The Prawn Season* (2002)
Adrian Blamires, *The Effect of Coastal Processes* (2005)
Adrian Blamires, *The Pang Valley* (2010)
Adrian Blamires & Peter Robinson (eds.), *The Arts of Peace* (2014)
Joseph Butler, *Hearthstone* (2006)
David Cooke, *A Murmuration* (2015)
Terry Cree, *Fruit* (2014)
Jane Draycott and Lesley Saunders, *Christina the Astonishing* (1998)
Jane Draycott, *Tideway* (2002)
John Froy, *Eggshell: A Decorator's Notes* (2007)
David Greenslade, *Zeus Amoeba* (2009)
A. F. Harrold, *Logic and the Heart* (2004)
A. F. Harrold, *Flood* (2009)
A. F. Harrold, *The Point of Inconvenience* (2013)
Ian House, *Cutting the Quick* (2005)
Ian House, *Nothing's Lost* (2014)
Gill Learner, *The Agister's Experiment* (2011)
Kate Noakes, *The Wall Menders* (2009)
Victoria Pugh, *Mrs Marvellous* (2008)
Peter Robinson, *English Nettles and Other Poems* (2010)
Peter Robinson (ed.), *Reading Poetry: An Anthology* (2011)
Peter Robinson (ed.), *A Mutual Friend: Poems for Charles Dickens* (2012)
Peter Robinson, *Foreigners, Drunks and Babies: Eleven Stories* (2013)
Lesley Saunders, *Her Leafy Eye* (2009)
Lesley Saunders, *Cloud Camera* (2012)
Susan Utting, *Houses Without Walls* (2006)
Susan Utting, *Fair's Fair* (2012)

Man with Bombe Alaska

Kate Behrens

TWO
RIVERS
PRESS

First published in the UK in 2016 by Two Rivers Press
7 Denmark Road, Reading RG1 5PA.
www.tworiverspress.com

© Kate Behrens 2016

The right of the poet to be identified as the author of the work
has been asserted by her in accordance with the Copyright,
Designs and Patents Act of 1988.

All rights reserved. No part of this publication may be reproduced,
stored in or introduced into a retrieval system, or transmitted,
in any form, or by any means (electronic, mechanical, photocopying,
recording or otherwise) without the prior written permission of
the publisher.

ISBN 978-1-909747-14-2

1 2 3 4 5 6 7 8 9

Two Rivers Press is represented in the UK by Inpress Ltd
and distributed by Central Books.

Cover design and illustration by Sally Castle.
Text design by Nadja Guggi and typeset in Janson and Parisine.

Printed and bound in Great Britain by Imprint Digital, Exeter.

Acknowledgements
Some of these poems, or earlier versions of them, have appeared
in *Blackbox Manifold* 9 and 13, *University of Reading Creative Arts
Anthology* 2013 and 2015, *Sitegeist* and *The Arts of Peace: An Anthology
of Poetry* (Two Rivers Press with the English Association, 2014).
I am grateful to their editors, and in particular to Adam Piette, and
to Peter Robinson for his help with this book.

In memory of my twin, Sophie Behrens
1959 – 1985

Contents

I

Original Song | 3
Black to White | 4
Relief | 5
Crochet Lesson (Italy 1973) | 6
Soundscape | 7
Madonna Blue | 8
The Grotto Smeraldo | 9
We Tread Forwards | 10
Last Cut, First Steps | 11
Better than Nothing | 12
Saints on a Rood Screen Dado | 13
Christmas Ghost | 14

II

After Birth | 17
Selective Memory | 18
Cliff Edge in Gozo | 19
Beyond Matters of Taste | 20
The Satellite's Mountain | 21
The Slow Learner | 22

III

Intact Arches | 25
Confusion | 26
Private Car | 27
Night Words | 28
Looking for Clues | 29
Outside la Musée de Préhistoire | 32

IV

The Swimmer | 35
Accident in my Old Village | 36
Paulette | 37
Killing Time | 38
Man with Bombe Alaska | 39
Mrs Penrose and Son | 40
Like an Open Book | 41
Leonard's War | 42

V

Two Fathers | 45
Painter with Eye-Patch | 46
The Opening End | 47
Tricky Colours | 48
Close Up | 49
Still Here | 50
The Beach | 51
Boanerges | 52
To my Father | 53
Termini with Cattle | 54

VI

Old Belongings | 57
A Millionairesse's Wood | 58
Conversation | 59
On Wittenham Clumps | 60
Lifelines | 61
Some Things I know Tonight | 62
If We Sell the House | 63
Natural Irregularities in the Surface | 64
The Blues and Old Golds | 65
Dark Star | 66

Original Song

The house has no
suspension; coach,
boat, whatever,
it peeps and rattles
for hours. Ozone
floods in on a
flickering wash;
bitter roses
scratch with tumbled
thorns. A fumbled
ragtime quickens
random flashes
round the booms.

We vanish up
a slow drawn breath.

Threads from the earth
mesh with furthest-
blown minor keys,
pale gold on deep
azurites. It's

a stilled darkness
for uncharted
harmonies to
wander on, through
dividing lines.

Six seconds long.

Black to White

(London/Turkey 1964)

1

You left, first, for a keyhole
of glass. Your breasts and ribs
slid under constellations.
Men pumped in the antidote.
Paraffin lamps were pink and green.

2

We knew it already
from flickering leaves.
The sea tucked in water-snakes,
brittle cicadas, also
the white sky. Nothing remained,
but hair, sand; some idea
of who you had been.

Relief

One spark, blood red. Spirea.
Just a refracted raindrop
on sun-struck humdrum leaves.
But it pulled on my skins' long
buried stars, once citrine, strung
on spines of orange lit snow,
or interstitial beacons
that fired green from a kerbstone,
all between death and a new home.

Diamond sharp, those fairies'
flashy transplantation
got us where no one ever died
for example, just in the nick of time.

.

Crochet Lesson (Italy 1973)

Our laps swam with mulberry leaves
(veils on bat-bitten streetlights
shivered over the school) –
she gathered up her crochet hook,
conjured the boys to perform for us,
seeded some new magenta web.
We played with *double entendres*
as her lurex hole developed
colours from a threatening sky.

They reined in their skidding machines,
hers, already skimmed off,
mine, the one on the loosest rails
who'd blasted us with bloodied riffs
festa nights in the *circolo*,
dismounting then, into the ring.
That sky of punched-up cherubims
crackled, boiled, then smelt of rain.

Circolo (It): club

Soundscape

Crossing, like those tattered mists'
distances we're unsure of,
a motor rips through drowsing spaces,
pins these layers down with a man
(never the tree slowly falling)

...but nearer, like deep sea divers
pumping the wall iris blue
or bundling onto a black cotton back
slow-picked herbs for caged rabbits,
people swishing through hip-length grass
bump on others' drowning voices...
Oxen breathe on each swing home.

Madonna Blue

Misfits on the tufts, stiff,
ant-bitten, we listen
as our battery-driven
Bach Violin Concertos
lift off. We have ptsd
undiagnosed, pencils,
paints, the up-rush when
Madonna blue accedes
Bach's warping phrases.

Stalks stick in elbows;
the fork in your weather's
pointed at unsayable
stuff. That swells, and small,
on last year's tilled soil,
the blundered into bowl
tips, then drains; I tickle
the grasses for brushes
blended by sun-blindness
into the furtive patterns
and feel of solid poisons.

It's not like déjà vue
but a thing transmuted
by me, hardly felt by you,
tangled in the looping
dangers of your head. I flee
what clings to a jittery
back-hander like haunting
memories here. Our healing
leaves you scattered, alone,
with paint tubes all over
the stopped concertos.

The Grotto Smeraldo

After the milk-skinned
shudder of Aegean,
jellied light
is sea's seeing eye.

We rock here, cradled
in its pupil.

Tutto è bello.

Chiaroscuro
draws a new line –
Amalfitano.

Horizons have turned
to the singular.

We'll clear the grotto,
dribble our bodies
into what flashes
ease up those mountains,
doubled, on approaching land.

We Tread Forwards

(October 1985)

Amongst yellow and blue spheres
(buttocks, bags, turbans, moons)
diamante, touched, looms red-hot
on the conscience – lychees
blur under the railway arch
where insolent skies gleam eyeball-white,
we tread forwards through bright puddles,
trail behind us almost three hours
(noted, along with a dead mouth's
reason to still utter words,
their reverberations,
as bats fly to unheard sounds)…

Nature startles in her sentence
now survivors see it's true.

Life's 'rich'. 'Miraculous'.

Last Cut, First Steps

Light in the hairline cracks
aromatic with basil-leaf oils
filtering into a chemical sleep –
that morning broke through with pearls
and words restrung on bearable breaths.

I don't remember the process of 'birth',
though that's what it seemed to be,
only the dizzying distillation
as hooking on some immaculate line
it bore its first steps with braveness

and the hammering quiet of ivy
flipping no message on glass.

Better than Nothing

It happens over and over, still –
you only went away for a while
your not-being ends, though
as when you threw all those silver coins
onto the rails in the Underground
or vanished when I drew too close
you are never surmountable,
deadness being the atmosphere
where these events are laid down
too ethereally for us both.

Saints on a Rood Screen Dado

You lie in an East wind
spinning off empty barley fields
in new pink saxifrage collar.

They can't provoke some absences,
and where a masterstroke began
ends in precarious lines

(four are almost entire
some half there
some in a kind of limbo) –

I guess, through criss-crossed light
your bones are just that,
a life's long pentimento

before your mouth enunciates,
adjusting to casual quiet
my near-future's insidious whisper.

It's like devotion's real purpose
makes me a listening absentee;
there's nothing but desirous colour

saying 'Ambrose', 'Augustine'
'Gregory', 'Jerome',
not 'there', but 'everywhere'.

Christmas Ghost

She's not by the estuary,
nor where a bird occludes
a birthplace of crippled pines
for clouds stiffened like nacre,
suggesting mortal dangers
or supernatural relief,

but under a tree with smashed glasses,
embers of chestnut smoking on,
the Boxing hours held in abeyance.

II

After Birth

The world left behind had shrunk to this
tryst mirrored by flinty sparks
coming from darkened spots on the globe;
the bold rock of your head
abandoned in sleep on a ribby field,
each intake of breath given
with seeming acquiescence
(whom belonged to whom and how
inside these curtains so confused
specifically for our forbearance)
before first words broke through.

Selective Memory

A man on a red banquette
prone in the summer of '94
pours tuna-water down his throat.
The lone dolphin, a female,
trawls that year's bay again
beyond your first carousel;
rain smells come off starlings,
fall from trees in Collioure.

I don't remember every failure,
yet in Barcelona
a dog in some walled garden
appears like a saviour,
coloured blonde and viridian
under the cherimoya.

Cliff Edge in Gozo

You in white dress, shaped like an X
marked three stripes. It was a great
composition, weighty as a De Stael
till scale then changing senses
had gusts upon you gobbling
what remained of sentences,
a bilious chiaroscuro
below your childish legs
and sea-splashed rocks looking up
to your whole flesh laughing
over the deep crevasse.
I ran across the salt pans, then –
El Greco melted back to De Stael,
to splashes of holiday colours
framed like those displays on walls'
traditional suggestions,
your shape to a kiss on ceruleans
describing sea and air.

Beyond Matters of Taste

…we returned to thickly-leaved glasses
flies on their edges
dead air
but stuck long after the Maghrib prayer
a sharp breath even the hardest
swallowed in the yellow medina
became a thing out there
belting out on ruined haunches
still more sound of mind;
the night desert reached out
to our sleep-curled fingers
and, there being no earthly point
in peace, the night unfolded.

The Satellite's Mountain

On our hedges blue-tits hang oddly.
England's false-exotic –
a gloss on the rotten wood
from terrible seasons
grows many tiny adventures.
A satellite image of Mount Hood
sails you down its wild paint-spills;
or some place where the ends drip,
the two of you'll be looking up plants –
or in Bagby Hot Springs
where no electricity
may explain this growing quiet?
How does the natural world
fight back trammeling highways?
Man's thumb's incontinent
under the rule of indexing fingers.
Computer screens between us
heighten the summer's tipping point.
I'll wait for your effulgence
to white out these awful hues.

The Slow Learner

The garden, lured into May
turns from tone to mortal
colour, all holiday-
bothered-by-premature-end.

But green-gold's resembling
a tone; it creeps towards calm
disallowed by others' pain.
The old bat scribbles again

what's clear in cloud eruptions;
best for them to let it in.

III

Intact Arches

When we got lost in Paradise Wood
you threw your sheepskin jacket
over a barbed-wire fence.
I watched you close to the post
climbing precisely
knowing your body's weight
knowing the wire.

You told me to take off my coat
and when I reached the top
I turned very slowly
fixing the lowing cows
a distant fire
the rising field, as markers.

Long after you'd left
I remembered a deer leaping
frame by frame through hanging creepers
the heap of rubble in the ruin
where we'd lain so far apart
watching the cattle grazing
through the chapels' intact arches
the other side of the valley.

Mostly I remember your palms
turning upwards, surprisingly small,
waiting to catch me if I fall.

Confusion

A man, who followed thoughts
fixed to his head like a torch,
half-blew past corner shops...

You could've taken me there
but wordless exchanges
were blocked, the very idea

nicked our freedom.
Police sirens kicked in,
the air thickened; the worst

and best revealed themselves;
silver black crumpled man
stumbled on crisp packets.

Private Car

Examine the verges' new weight
of past-its-best cow-parsley,
approaching a mistaken suburb,
a tilted bride caught through trees
having her skirts twitched,
some fortuitous swan's glide
into the black frame. That bare nerve
after the lights turn red
holds down depths of froth,
and after they cross, more purple twists
wired on, more gleaming domes,
staccato in the traffic jam,
in exhaust-cloud shimmer,
repeats, and as others' desires
insistent summons to my shame
picks them out with yellow lines.

Then after the route's corrected,
the birds and bees getting-it-on
in homely bushes of evening fragrance
are full of small savagery,
small recompense.

Night Words

Words from this peripheral world
trip you to stumble awake,
one clear sentence on buffeting thermals

…'people drop pebbles in wells
with that same guileless hope
behind your confidences'…

Then the motorbike on the trails
night left startles birds,
and re-examining decibels
metered out by dozy hopefuls
(the blurred lace of their better talk
hardening as nest material)
I stalk a morning instead of your face,
wait for the sigh of a bus to release us,
flocks of words trapped in nets,
more slowly – this un-knowingness;
eyelids to your wide horizon.

Looking For Clues

For the sculptor, Peter Foster

        1

The two-year old in chequered shoes
lifts the fine arch of her brows
over an orange chair-back
from under a jammy corona
light as one of your blue-tits' nests.
Later as I'm listening out
to sounds an oyster might whistle,
she wheels her pram and doll
past the water dispenser,
waves goodbye to everyone
and the verdigris air's an envelope
sealing itself on her sap.

        2

You're forced to miss a flying bird
(now the same as everything else,
stark as words left in the air).

The steel frame flickers
with all your old belongings.

I steer you by an unfathomable
tenderness in your rigid arm,
past the hospital book stall

and even the barrier
freeing us to the roundabout
just grew livelier…

3

Half-numb from a yellow glaze
we'd plodded in smells of unshed sap
losing integrity, into the dusk...
Was it serendipity then,
tumbling a glaucous flash
and arsenal fashioned from black and blue play

to this, a rare interpreter
of raven glossolalia,
or that a raven remembered you?

4

Close to a quiet crater
chert fists are winking scarlet.
There's blood in the eye of the forest
though green blackens it,
larches phosphoresce
and some thin cataract's
uncertainly scrawled over
right to the tips of skeleton oaks,
just under a human's lines.

You've got the medicine
river and voice prescribed;
sloe, ash, pungent ribes –
here, this burnt out hollow
where we'll find morels.

5

On the slope we're into Carthusians –
toenails as blue as indigo
touch the thrown-out chalk.
You stop, tickle some Dame's Violet,

remark that in this ditch your toe
was where at 2 a.m. last night
a glowworm lit your path,
how baby tawnys sssss'd you off,
and later, in Hill Road,
tongue loosened further by hedges,
'let's trip these cyclists into tomorrow',
followed by dreams of Father Pio,
your recipe for pilchard soup
and all the possible things to do
with neam...

I'm drifting as counties of women
hail prayers down your scars.

Outside La Musée de Préhistoire

(for Harriet Frazer)

Paleolithic man
cluttered the chateau environs
with liver-coloured 'livres de beurre'
here, where Star of Bethlehem
and that past we barely touched on
seem entangled for a moment –

then, with remembered flowers, flints,
a path's clear eye on the stream,
you realise nothing had darkened a thing,
like a glimpse of prehistory
on that very morning,
you'd no doubt see again.

Livres de beurre (Fr); pounds of butter; Neolithic flint cores found around Le Grand Pressigny, France.

IV

The Swimmer

She's bold as a seal
for no reason. Her head
scatters an upside-down bridge,
the disused chapel,
a bar where drunk husband
fumbles for pen.
She ploughs through blue sky-scraps,
settles on doubled reeds
small as a coot's nest
inside the mountain.

Accident in my Old Village

Held by your body's weight
in their dark noon house
you will be assaulted
as festa preparations
creep back up your staircase

(remembering their graces,
sounds that rose through floors,
marked us like orange sauces,
flight stains on outside walls
of angels, bats, angelus)…

and in such dark noon heat
folded in and on themselves,
reflections on your loggia glass
may be older pains released
deep inside the house's heart.

You'll see, time will pass.

Paulette

Paulette shows us her neighbour's attic.
Aged seventy-eight, in trousers,
she holds the ladder carelessly,
looks with eyes swollen by nothing.

The empty house is full of promise;
they will get back from Paris,
transform it with their bon esprit –
they will bring it back to life.

This is what you're guessing at.
Her thoughts are in absentia,
voice approximate,
but you know the English couple.

In an enclosed courtyard
muguets rest in a world
she has already dispensed with.
Smiling, she lets us in.

She says to her empty table,
'je ne vais pas bien',
and our vague hand-gestures
next to her boy's photograph

fall onto patterned vinyl.
There's no reason not to cry
at our last adieu, though we've rarely spoken.
Branches float like flotsam and jetsam.

Spring has come to the Indres et Loire.
Nothing will hold it from marching on.

Killing Time

After a fashion, where past
stands in for present tensions,
they stroll towards a ha-ha,
a summer-swollen silver,
that his arm might stretch,
encircle, on suffering wood
shadows lost in flesh
from high bulwarks
or their lives' vicissitudes –
and it does look, from afar
clear as daydreams, lazing
under summer's final blast.

However much it costs him,
that was another era
and from this unfolding view
recent stuff slants to nature,
develops on a softened breeze;
the here-and-now's apparent 'hush!'
so adjustments might be eased
moments longer (traffic rushes
blot out glimpsed clearings,
pile up, like dead things) –

whatever did or didn't happen,
the sun's already setting here.

Man with Bombe Alaska

Look, but it's doubts' flashes only
dying inside a chilly woman –
yes, she'll pass on the huge bombe,
dribbles of burnt jam, as he considers
what's blown over on his side
with conscientious stabs,
everything disfigured and froth…

She'd dip a spoon in his new-mint eyes
for their many drunk cherries,
though deep in the cool of them
an unhappy spike of sweetness
trips her up and into the Ladies
to monitor hurts, preserve what remains
of a lipsticked reserve mother blew on her brain,
a fudged u-turn to always rely on,
now cheap strawberry fool in the glass
after Champagne, the shared bill's last proof
that she's a stupid cow,
less human than his dazzle…

Mrs Penrose and Son

Tom found her panting, rattled
by juggernauts on irksome winds
and hazed glinting distances
bring back their early battles.

She's gone for semi-blindness
in the way that lovers can
when too much time's just been blown
he's thinking, as the misted eyes
clear with three Drambuies –
(her light economies
split by a bluish façade
switch to bifurcated glow).

Eyes don't look like windows, though.
She's thinking, 'deadhead roses
after he's gone' as some owl
rocks dusk for whole mountains
of endangered young;
then, 'there's nothing to be done'.

She'll take off the barbed wire crown,
stand toward the open sea,
waders calling.

Like an Open Book

This nurse with hypodermic
bustles round uncharted
damage under aged skin,
bunched up too with smiling
at punched lines on ceiling tiles,

says, (all x-ray eyes
leaning in, like no disguise
or made up personae'd
ever escape her beam),
'your face tells a story',
nicks slaphappy dreams
as one might a burn blister.

No turning back then
from what was written down.
Too late to block it out with brown.

Leonard's War

'Greta, you can't, thankfully, see
I'm yellow as a daffodil! I wasn't, you know,
cut-out for tanks by nature, it's stifling in desert heat,
visibility practically zero,

the worst was dripping all over the gunner
(who's kindly steering my elbow now) –
those five offending articles there
look harmless when you're safely out

you'd've been sympathetic, dear –

these kind chaps are holding me up,
(though legs appear to be buckling under),
maybe you'd laugh at my lurid colour

something in my waistcoat pocket,
she's lit-up in Regent Street

stretching away, bowler hats,

Libertys' lights, her slant
on things, in deep
snow

she's wearing the cashmere coat I gave her

it's jumbled-up in a cold sweat

agrees I was not culpable
for this small mishap

foreign fiascos, but love got me out

this far ...'

V

Two Fathers

The old man's clearing his throat.
Evening is weighted
with box, Albertine flowers.
Flies buzz on billowing lace.
Dad's still persona non grata.

We're in a kind of two-poster
and Ethel screams 'Eth–el'
out of the cedar branches.

Cedars look like peacock tails.
We don't get all the poems.
His dangerous eyes
water at Shelley and Byron.

He could be a traffic light.

Painter with Eye-Patch

The peninsula's clutch on a
sea-front's better days
(yours, queasy in old arcades)
leans towards those dithyrambs
tumbled off white-lipped rollers...

The other side's a light marina,
bloodied suns in *mirador*s
or Santiago, smoothed to a boulder
blinded by admirers' palms,
locked in with steepened black.

You inch about rehearsed flashes,
test familiar ground, stick-mark
a sudden wetness. Glaring cars,
now travellers, are smeared
invitations to slip, right here
on Calle San Andrés

before the Bar Rosalía,
your table, almost a-flutter
with the sine qua non of
Luis's absolute discretion
and votary's eye for empties.

Remember, as a jaundiced child
how a very yellowed lightness
turned off cherry-blossom pinks?

mirador (Sp); (enclosed) balcony

The Opening End

Headlights pick on those saplings
seeded in a blackened aisle
we'd glimpsed through gaps in masonry.

It might've ended in that nights'
kaleidoscopic marinas,
or, hours later, wavy lines,
as watery eyes and nose
seek out the last bar alive
and half-promised pink emerges
heavy as wings over your headland,
the cow tied to a zed bend
lowing like there's no tomorrow –
pink, all through the burnt smell.

Tricky Colours

You're sure, for a moment, a sultry blue shocks the hill
though yellow-bellied clouds – look with your only eye –
drag a decent sky-dream down, are over-arched with dolphin grey.
I've had to be realistic (should I call this clump
'love', 'wicked', 'mad'?) A cold wind blows. Weak sun
flicks bald earth, cups the ants-nests' shrunken rock-rose leaves –
snowdrifts are forecast for mid-evening.

What answers rests imagined too – you'll see, in the crook of this tree
moss lit by a dying suns' tricks.

Close Up

It felt like a tic, regardless, in mine
as I slipped past a light welcome
of palmate leaves and suitcase stripes –
fixed to the sobering wall, an eye,
fallen away from swollen drifts
of humans, gulls, heavy machines
blown up here as company.
Miles from my own round the door's reveal.

Still, it seems I threaten your peace,
and shyness-to-shyness insists
that each hurt's glanced imprint
patterns white inches between us
with living stains that look like love
depending on your line of vision.

I'm afraid we're here again
(because we think you're dying).

Still Here

Here, in this obscurity,
as you lie like your bones too-
imaginable flesh departed already
some days ago, the heavy
machinery meshes with voices and sighs,
the curtain's swelling on,
a soft sea breeze; your eyes
are alive still,
fixed on the edge of the sobering wall.

The Beach

Beside the Atlantic, the girls
lay out their towels like days of the week.
Your walls are evening-coloured
hung with others' bright pictures.

They spread their painted toes;
the season smells of frying fish.
Your head's beached, full of holes,
still like unbridgeable rock.

Topless breasts are curlicues
up and down the glass hotels.
Your flesh has left you fragile,
bones to drape a blanket on.

A man with tennis racquet
has yellow-bikini jumping up.
Get it right or let it rest
where you're hanging on, love.

The sand goes road-kill beige
under suitable footwear.
You dream-laugh as always,
babble at the on-comer.

Though it has no vegetation,
the beach, it waits for dawn.

Boanerges

In the dark, I sat with the worn block –
Santiago, not pitch-black,
with dumbed-down head and mouth-less,
was more a 'Boanerges',
Jesus' nickname for him.

Silica facets winked off
caressed dents in his bulk.
The steep corner where cars braked,
lesser carvings affronted him,
broke in on headlight strips.

His breast smelt of iron.
He'd see no better for eyes,
speak no louder for proper lips.

To my Father

'You look like my daughter Kate but your voice is different'

These cloud mountains have split.
Meteorologists
get why some tops detach,
float along parallel tracks
high above your hospital.

I counted fluctuations
in the thickets of your chest
for three nights, mumbled when
clearer drifts from your mouth
recognized my wetted cloth.

It was some phenomena
from what is left unbroken,
easily forgotten
as clouds from a plane, so long
as it's you remembering.

Your recovered youth has gone.
Not this remembered child.

Termini With Cattle

1

Arriving home, the lit up cows
blacken the grass
under the lime in a tableau –
half dark chewed bushes
startle to close-up heads
forcing the boundary edges,
and exhausted leaves
steaming on breaths the cool
air – flies on the architraves of their eyes
sting, as bovine coughs sting you,
unnoticed by midnight men
waiting for the slaughter,
shake up their moonlit shapes.

2

Thoughts of a mountain pool –
a double-edged Umbria
patterned then, at last
with copied ilex leaves,
black behind snow-white muzzles,
flashily repeated gazes,
only the sky aware, here
of the creams Piero
would have made like strata of limestone;
and mum's friend, the doctor,
right foot half buried in shale,
filling in cicadas'
chained song with factual remnants.
Packages of foreleg,
odd shipwrecked haunches
only addressed that dry background,
echo in monochrome
down these restless lines.

VI

Old Belongings

I dig at their dumbed down words,
milk-glass bottle shoulders.
The middle of a kettle
belly-laughs. Like what's missed here
was rubbish. You'd think it their
ghosts pointing out hungers:
old-man's-beard scrawled on the
cherry's small élan, whitebeams
sucked in and held for silver
on breezes out from nowhere.
That would be wrong. Disturbed
are old longings
simply to belong.

A Millionairesse's Wood

The wood grows back from that lustrous
pre-storm light to opening quiet,
a crowd of dark euphorbia
hooking the south face, everything else

a steep layer of chemical powders
eyes map at frilled edges,
as wide in-betweens allow
colour to flower in stark silvers –

after an ash creaks once,
echoes of campaniles
fill with jackdaws, invisible bells,
fall back, into these earthworks

where we peer into the pale
of forced-up dead leaves.

Conversation

Up on the spar
(just where it tilts
and swoops far to changeable bosk),
a grouping of poisonous darkness
gathers the four half-nude birches
into indefinite conversation,
showing with evergreen oiliness
how vulnerable were their golden coins,
how very naked their silver flesh,
and smooth under a startled moon.
Crazily upright, in truth
and on the steep gradient,
the birches only answer as mirrors,
as if bewitched by their own mothers
into unnatural softness.

On Wittenham Clumps

Down the escarpment deeper than iron-age,
it bats about on a composite picture,
filched, I see, from 'Dinosaur Habitats',
where I was swamp-god in eras of terror
fixing a scale-less relationship
in black and white on waxed grey paper,
beneath an array of orderly
jungle leaves – this time, it blurs,
gladly, where you might nail it
for research into Wittenham Clumps,
between the red and yellow plum trees
branching on kite-fliers' clouds.

Lifelines

Silence rocks this whole
community of birds;
in crystals, their search
develops profound threads
stitching the garden to itself
and boundary hedge
of dubious comforts – snow
is ladled on everything.
In sub-zeros, they breathe out
measurable warmth
where imagination freezes,
bind you with a drawn line
again and again as dawn breaks
to their smudged horizon.

Some Things I Know Tonight

These night smells quicken false promises.

Skinless people have x-ray eyes.

How to grow ridge cucumbers.

To test if pasta's al dente
fling it against the kitchen tiles.

Madness is knowing for sure.

Something about the unstable –
how wrecking them back to unmoved stages
makes them less hazardous.

Vaseline on the nostrils
relieves allergic rhinitis.

A being moves in the wilderness bit.

Asymmetrical lines
feed the heart salt truths.

Everyone likes a list.

Shames' lessons are always obeyed.

Fennel seeds go with livers.

The garden is tubed with over-sexed flowers.

We travel each other's waves in silence.

Diving is a secretive sport.

If We Sell the House

Seen through an open sash,
the lime against cloud cliffs
is just frail leaves,
the blue cows' breaths and
waking eyes blank drift
though separating,
still enmeshed, silvered
by a bright moon.

Natural Irregularities in the Surface

Pinned to the furrows
by gibbous moon at tails' end,
orange starburst at their heads,
one flaps. A gap in this low
relief leaves them unmoved,
strung along the field's rib.
Its face is unreadable,
wings enthralled.

The Blue and Old Golds

In quiet and evening
those clicks point to blue-tits
cracking up first skins
of sound with larch cones –

clearer, as jet graze blooms,
new layers of whispered song
join resins weeping to
ginger up casualties
immodestly blown down
into another's
frail end branches.

Dark Star

Information under-load.
Look to this fish belly sky,
above, to a dark star…

It could be a pointed blindness
follows the echo of footfall,
an end to unblinking lights.

Six frosted larches soar
where you have no idea
what measures are needed…

The everyday lives of others
you'd find unmanageable.

I've long stepped like callipers
over your sparkling ground
and repetitions, substrata

look so vulgar down here.
The quiet curtains are pulled.

Solitude holds your brightness, still.

We are this distant from growing old.

Two Rivers Press has been publishing in and about Reading since 1994. Founded by the artist Peter Hay (1951–2003), the press continues to delight readers, local and further afield, with its varied list of individually designed, thought-provoking books.